OUR FAVORITE VIDEO GAMES

TETRIS

BY KIERAN DOWNS

EPIC

BELLWETHER MEDIA ❖ MINNEAPOLIS, MN

EPIC

EPIC BOOKS are no ordinary books. They burst with intense action, high-speed heroics, and shadows of the unknown. Are you ready for an Epic adventure?

This is not an official *Tetris* book. It is not approved by or connected with The Tetris Company, Inc.

This edition first published in 2026 by Bellwether Media, Inc.

No part of this publication may be reproduced in whole or in part without written permission of the publisher. For information regarding permission, write to Bellwether Media, Inc., Attention: Permissions Department, 3500 American Blvd W, Suite 150, Bloomington, MN 55431.

Library of Congress Cataloging-in-Publication Data

Names: Downs, Kieran, author.
Title: Tetris / by Kieran Downs.
Description: Minneapolis, MN : Bellwether Media, Inc., 2026. | Series: Our favorite video games | Includes bibliographical references and index. | Audience: Ages 7-12 | Audience: Grades 4-6 | Summary: "Engaging images accompany information about Tetris. The combination of high-interest subject matter and light text is intended for students in grades 2 through 7"-- Provided by publisher.
Identifiers: LCCN 2025003626 (print) | LCCN 2025003627 (ebook) | ISBN 9798893045062 (library binding) | ISBN 9798893047356 (paperback) | ISBN 9798893046441 (ebook)
Subjects: LCSH: Tetris (Game)--Juvenile literature.
Classification: LCC GV1469.37 .D683 2026 (print) | LCC GV1469.37 (ebook) | DDC 794.8--dc23/eng/20250213
LC record available at https://lccn.loc.gov/2025003626
LC ebook record available at https://lccn.loc.gov/2025003627

Text copyright © 2026 by Bellwether Media, Inc. EPIC and associated logos are trademarks and/or registered trademarks of Bellwether Media, Inc. Bellwether Media is a division of FlutterBee Education Group.

Editor: Christina Leaf   Designer: Gabriel Hilger

Printed in the United States of America, North Mankato, MN.

TABLE OF CONTENTS

A BIG WIN	4
THE HISTORY OF *TETRIS*	8
TETRIS TODAY	16
TETRIS FANS	20
GLOSSARY	22
TO LEARN MORE	23
INDEX	24

A BIG WIN

A player is in the top 10 of a game of *Tetris 99*. The blocks are falling fast. But the player stays calm. They drop a block at the perfect time. Four lines disappear! They win!

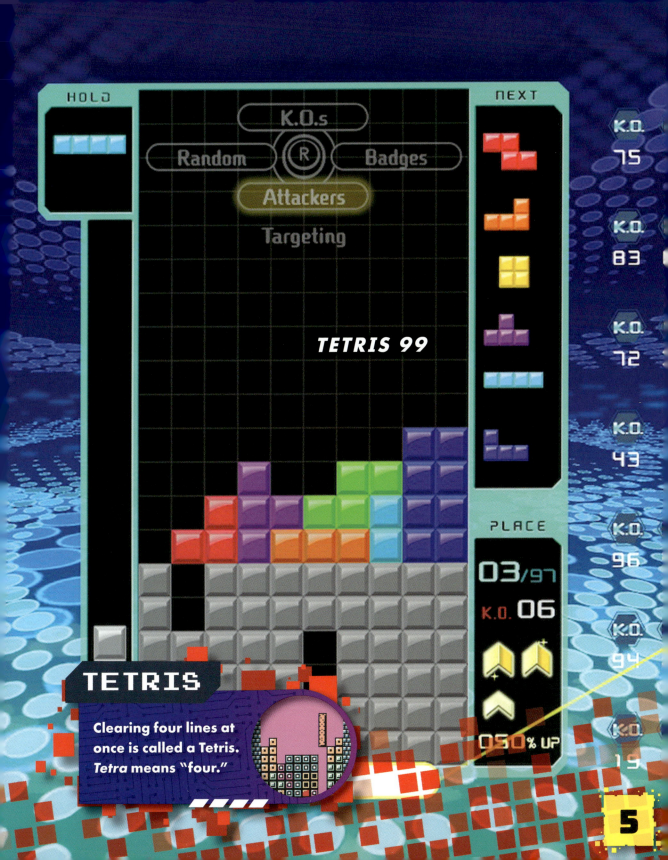

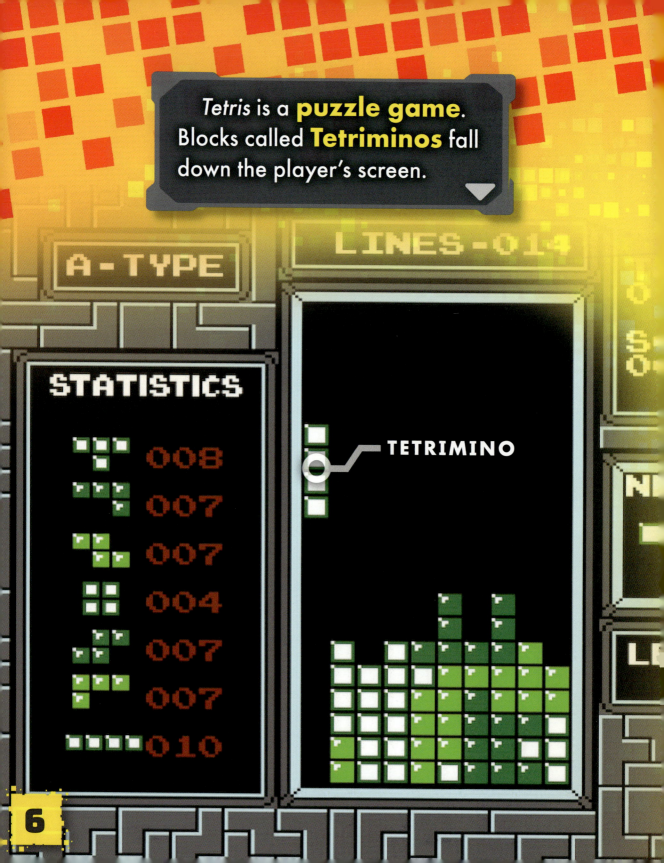

THE HISTORY OF TETRIS

ALEXEY PAJITNOV

Tetris was first made by Alexey Pajitnov in 1984. The game quickly spread across the **Soviet Union**.

A businessman named Henk Rogers found the game in 1988. He created a version for the Nintendo Famicom in Japan.

MUSIC

The song used in *Tetris* is a Russian folk tune. It is called "Korobeiniki."

NINTENDO FAMICOM

CREATOR PROFILE

NAME	Alexey Pajitnov
BIRTHPLACE	Moscow, Soviet Union
BIRTHDAY	April 16, 1955
OTHER GAMES	Hexic, Marbly, Faces, Hatris

In 1989, Pajitnov and Rogers agreed to let Nintendo release a Tetris game.

Nintendo sold it as a **pack-in** with the Game Boy. The game was a hit! Over 35 million copies were sold.

IN SPACE

In 1993, *Tetris* became the first video game played in space!

Many Tetris games came out on **consoles** and computers in the 1990s.

12

In 2006, *Tetris DS* came out. It sold over two million copies! *Tetris Party* came out in 2008. It was a hit on the Wii.

Tetris was also on **mobile devices**. In 2006, Tetris for iPod came out. Tetris for iPhone followed in 2008. It had over 100 million downloads by 2010!

In 2014, Tetris was named one of the top-selling video games of all time!

TETRIS TIMELINE

1984

Alexey Pajitnov creates *Tetris*

1989

Tetris for the Game Boy is a hit

2006

Tetris DS is released

2014

Tetris is named one of the top-selling video games of all time

2019

Tetris 99 is released

TETRIS TODAY

Today, *Tetris* can be played on many devices. These include consoles, computers, and mobile devices.

TETRIS GAMES BY SALES

BIG SELLER

All Tetris games together have sold 520 million units!

- TETRIS (GAME BOY): 35 MILLION
- TETRIS (NES): 5.58 MILLION
- TETRIS DS: 2.74 MILLION
- TETRIS DX: 1.88 MILLION
- PUYO PUYO TETRIS (ALL): 1.4 MILLION

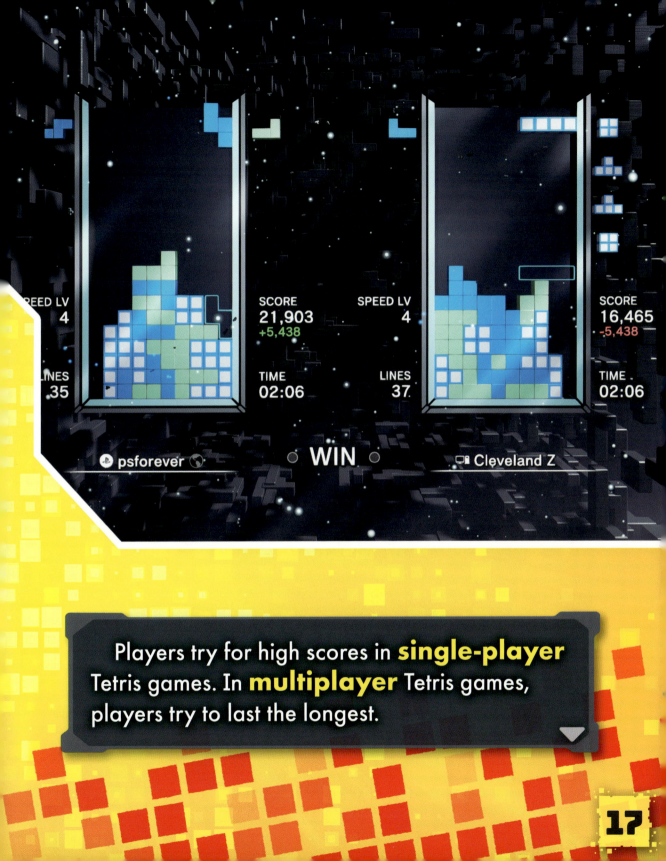

Players try for high scores in **single-player** Tetris games. In **multiplayer** Tetris games, players try to last the longest.

There are more than 200 versions of *Tetris*. *Tetris 99* pits 99 players against each other. The last one standing wins!

TETRIS 99

BIG SCREEN

Tetris has been played on buildings! The lights on the buildings made the shapes.

Tetris Effect can be played using **virtual reality**. Players can stack up **combos** with the "Zone" feature.

VIRTUAL REALITY

TETRIS EFFECT

SPEED LV
3

LINES
27 / 36

ZONE

TIME
04:16

AREA SCORE
5,294

19

TETRIS FANS

Fans can buy Tetris-themed clothes. There are even Tetris snacks!

Skilled *Tetris* players can **compete** at the Classic Tetris World **Championship**. There are many ways for players to enjoy *Tetris*!

CLASSIC TETRIS WORLD CHAMPIONSHIP

DATE once per year

LOCATION around the United States

EVENT a championship for classic *Tetris* players

GLOSSARY

championship—a contest to decide the best team or person

combos—series of points in a row

compete—to work for something for which another person is also working

consoles—game systems that connect to TVs to play video games

mobile devices—devices such as smartphones or tablets that can be used on the go

multiplayer—related to games that are able to be played by more than one player at a time

pack-in—a game that is sold with a console

puzzle game—a game that challenges players to solve a puzzle before they can reach the next level

single-player—related to games played by one person

Soviet Union—a country in eastern Europe and western Asia that existed from 1922 to 1991

Tetriminos—blocks made up of four squares used in *Tetris*

virtual reality—computer technology that makes users feel like they are somewhere else

TO LEARN MORE

AT THE LIBRARY

Galanin, Dennis. *The Amazing World of Video Game Development*. Sanger, Calif.: Familius, 2022.

Neuenfeldt, Elizabeth. *Video Games*. Minneapolis, Minn.: Bellwether Media, 2023.

Shaw, Gina. *What Is Nintendo?* New York, N.Y.: Penguin Workshop, 2021.

ON THE WEB

Factsurfer.com gives you a safe, fun way to find more information.

1. Go to www.factsurfer.com.

2. Enter "Tetris" into the search box and click 🔍.

3. Select your book cover to see a list of related content.

INDEX

Classic Tetris World Championship, 20, 21
clothes, 20
computers, 12, 16
consoles, 8, 9, 11, 12, 13, 16
fans, 20
history, 8, 10, 11, 12, 13, 14
Japan, 8
lines, 4, 5, 7
mobile devices, 14, 16
multiplayer, 17
Nintendo, 8, 9, 10, 11
Pajitnov, Alexey, 8, 9, 10
player, 4, 6, 7, 17, 18, 19, 20
puzzle game, 6
Rogers, Henk, 8, 10
sales, 11, 13, 14, 16

single-player, 17
snacks, 20
song, 9
Soviet Union, 8
Tetriminos, 6, 7
Tetris 99, 4, 5, 18
Tetris DS, 13
Tetris Effect, 19
Tetris Party, 13
timeline, 15
versions, 18
virtual reality, 19

The images in this book are reproduced through the courtesy of: Dmytro Sunagatov/ AdobeStock, front cover; Gringer/ Wikipedia, p. 3; skvalval, p. 4; Kieran Downs, p. 5; Gabriel Hilger, pp. 5 (fact), 6, 9 (music), 16, 19 (*Tetris Effect*); Damian Yerrick/ Wikipedia, pp. 7, 15; Wojtek Laski/ Contributor/ Getty Images, p. 8; alswart/ AdobeStock, p. 9 (TV); ArcadeImages/ Alamy Stock Photo, p. 9 (*Tetris*); Evan-Amos/ Wikipedia, p. 9 (Nintendo Famicom); CTK/ Alamy Stock Photo, p. 9 (Alexey Pajitnov); amoly/ AdobeStock, p. 10 (Game Boy); dannyburn/ AdobeStock, pp. 10 (cartridge), 15 (cartridge); Jordi Villar, p. 11 (Game Boy playing *Tetris*); El Barto/ Flickr, p. 11 (Game Boy *Tetris* pack-in); Russell Hart/ Alamy Stock Photo, p. 12 (in space); StockPhotoPro/ AdobeStock, pp. 12-13; Hugh Threlfall/ Alamy Stock Photo, p. 13 (Nintendo DS); zxcvbnm/ Wikipedia, pp. 13 (*Tetris DS*), 15 (*Tetris DS*); kern bridges/ Alamy Stock Photo, p. 14 (*Tetris* iPhone); nathsegato/ AdobeStock, p. 14 (iPod); Simonlc/ Wikipedia, p. 14 (*Tetris* iPod); L ke/ Wikipedia, p. 15 (*Tetris 99*); *Tetris Effect*, p. 17; Nicole Lienemann/ AdobeStock, p. 18 (Nintendo Switch); Jack Guez/ Staff/ Getty Images, p. 18 (big screen); whyframeshot/ AdobeStock, p. 19 (virtual reality); 3df/ Wikipedia, p. 20; Lawrence K. Ho/ Contributor/ Getty Images, p. 21 (Classic *Tetris* World Championship); picture alliance/ Contributor/ Getty Images, p. 21 (Tetris snacks); Tatiana Popova, p. 23.